ALLIGATOR WRESTLING AND YOU

An Impractical Guide
to an Impossible Sport

Other Avon Camelot Books by
Louis Phillips

ASK ME ANYTHING ABOUT THE PRESIDENTS

The closest thing LOUIS PHILLIPS has come to real-life alligator wrestling has been walking his seven-year-old twin sons to school. Not to be deterred from sharing advice to whomever will listen, he loves writing books about subjects he knows nothing about. If you don't believe us, ask his millions of fans. While waiting for his life to become a major motion picture, Mr. Phillips stands in front of mailboxes awaiting large royalty checks from his publishers. His other book for Avon Camelot is *Ask Me Anything About the Presidents*.

ALLIGATOR WRESTLING ANDYOU

An Impractical Guide to an Impossible Sport

LOUIS PHILLIPS

Illustrated by Valerie Costantino

AN AVON CAMELOT BOOK

ALLIGATOR WRESTLING AND YOU: AN IMPRACTICAL GUIDE TO AN IMPOSSIBLE SPORT is an original publication of Avon Books. This work has never before appeared in book form. This is a work of fiction. Any similarity to actual persons or events is purely coincidental.

AVON BOOKS
A division of
The Hearst Corporation
1350 Avenue of the Americas
New York, New York 10019

Copyright © 1992 by Louis Phillips
Illustrations by Valerie Costantino
Published by arrangement with the author
ISBN: 0-380-76303-6
RL: 6.3

First Avon Camelot Printing: July 1992

CAMELOT TRADEMARK REG. U.S. PAT. OFF. AND IN OTHER COUNTRIES, MARCA REGISTRADA, HECHO EN U.S.A.

Printed in the U.S.A.

OPM   10   9   8   7   6   5   4   3   2   1

for Tom, Mary, Daniel, and Jonathan Frosch

*You never know when a book like this
will come in handy*

CONTENTS

Foreword
xi

1.
How Do You Tell the Difference
Between a Real Live Alligator
and a Can of Peas?
1

2.
How Can I Practice Alligator Wrestling
If I Don't Have an Alligator
to Wrestle With?
9

3.
How to Tell Your Parents
That You Are Bringing Home
a Live Alligator
So That You Can Practice Your Wrestling Holds
17

4.

What to Name Your Alligator
25

5.

What to Feed Your Alligator
27

6.

Where to Wrestle with Your Alligator
31

7.

How to Turn Your Room
into a Swamp
43

8.

What to Wear While
Wrestling Your Alligator
47

9.

Alligators and the
Age-Old Cheerleader Question
55

10.

How to Tell an Alligator
from a Crocodile
60

11.

On Entering the Ring
Where a Live Alligator Awaits You
62

12.

What Not to Do While
Wrestling an Alligator
65

13.

How to Tickle an Alligator
67

14.

The Basic Moves
71

Conclusion
78

FOREWORD

What is the best and safest way of wrestling an alligator? That, of course, is the question upon everybody's lips. No matter what country I visit, people (men, women, children, and some man-eating plants) rush up to me with a plea upon their lips: "Please! I want to learn how to wrestle an alligator. Can you help me?"

Can I help them?

Are you kidding? I myself have never wrestled an alligator, and I have no intention of doing so. But after thinking about the problem and after facing a stack of unpaid bills I have decided, in spite of my lack of personal experience, to lay out a course of instruction for the absolute beginner. My theory is: Experience isn't everything.

That is why I am where I am today.

Where am I today? Ah, that is another question. To get the answer to that one, you will have to buy another book. In the meantime, for some strange reason, you are stuck with this one. So if you want to wrestle an alligator, there is no sense in beating around the bush.

Onward to chapter one!

(All right, if you wish to beat around the bush, go right ahead, but if there's an alligator lurking in the undergrowth, don't come crying to me about it. I've got problems of my own.)

ALLIGATOR WRESTLING AND YOU

An Impractical Guide to an Impossible Sport

CHAPTER ONE

How Do You Tell the Difference Between a Real Live Alligator and a Can of Peas?

It is sad but true: Alligators do not grow on trees. Repeat those six words to yourself at least ten times each day:

Alligators do not grow on trees.
Alligators do not grow on trees.
Alligators do not grow on trees.
Alligators do not grow on trees.
Alligators do not grow on trees.
Alligators do not grow on trees.
Alligators do not grow on trees.
Alligators do not grow on trees.
Alligators do not grow on trees.
Alligators do not grow on trees.

1

At first thought you might jump to the conclusion that it is an oversight upon the part of Nature, or a bad thing for the human race, that alligators do not grow on trees. A few moments of deep reflection, however, will make you realize that it is a very good thing that alligators do not grow on trees.

Suppose there had been an alligator tree in the Garden of Eden? Suppose, instead of an apple, Eve had picked an alligator off the tree, and suppose that alligator had eaten her up? Then where would the human race be?

Or suppose the famous scientist Sir Isaac Newton had been sitting under an alligator tree and not an apple tree. Suppose an alligator had dropped from the tree and had fallen onto the man's head? Sir Isaac Newton might have been crushed. At the very least he would have had a terrible headache for months on end. And then what would have happened to his discovery of gravity? Without gravity we would all be floating around in midair.

Imagine trying to read a book as difficult and thought-provoking as this one while floating around in midair. Nonsense. Stuff and nonsense.

FACT: Apple trees are beneficial to the human race; alligator trees are not.

If alligators grew on trees, you could go to the store and buy alligator juice. Aren't you lucky that no one is asking you to squeeze an alligator to make juice?

If there were such a drink as alligator juice, then you could make the Alligator Juice Cocktail:

½ cup of cranberry juice

½ cup of alligator juice

a wedge of lime

1 tablespoon of sugar

Pour over ice. Serve shaken, not stirred.

Do you know how many alligators you would have to squeeze in order to get a half cup of alligator juice? You don't? Good. Neither do I.

Of course, it might not be necessary to

squeeze alligators by hand. A brilliant scientist might invent the automatic alligator squeezer.

Now that it has been firmly established and you have been firmly convinced (we hope) that alligators do not grow on trees, two questions might pop into mind:

Just where do alligators come from?

How can I find an alligator to wrestle with?

(You might ask yourself why you are reading this book in the first place, but that question is beyond our jurisdiction.)

Let us examine one question at a time.

First, just where do alligators come from? The answer is that nobody knows. Oh sure, scientists may try to tell you about alligators mating and laying eggs, but not only can you not buy alligator juice in a grocery store, there is not one supermarket in America that will sell you a dozen alligator eggs. If alligator eggs were so abundant, we would be eating scrambled alligator eggs for breakfast.

The truth of the matter is this: One day you are walking down the street and there are no alligators to be seen. The next day you walk down that very same street and there you are—with hundreds of alligators holding up traffic and causing all sorts of commotion.

Or let us suppose that you have been sleeping in the same bed for ten or twelve years. Every night you fall asleep and there is no alligator in your bed. And then one night you wake up and there is an alligator sleeping beside you. It happens sometimes. Who can explain why?

Not me.

Besides, if you really cared where alligators came from, wouldn't you have discovered the answer before now? Why would you wait for me to come along and do all the work?

P.S. Now that you have read this far, I suppose you think you deserve an answer to the question: How do you tell the difference between a real live alligator and a can of peas? OK, OK, just don't nag me. A can of peas has a label on it. Alligators in the wild are not labeled. Peas are small, round, and green. Alligators are not.

There. Now on to the second question of our philosophical inquiry.

CHAPTER TWO

How Can I Practice Alligator Wrestling
If I Don't Have an Alligator
to Wrestle With?

Now we come to the second question:

How can I find an alligator to wrestle with?

This indeed is a difficult question to answer, a question that has stumped the best minds of my generation. Your generation too, I might add. After all, you are probably thinking to yourself—and is there any better way to think? How can I practice alligator wrestling if I don't have an alligator to practice with?

First (and this secret is worth the price of

this book twenty times over!) **You do not need an alligator in order to practice alligator wrestling**. A younger brother or sister will do. Or, if you do not have a younger brother or sister, or if a younger brother or sister does not wish to cooperate, you can always use any of the following:

> a lawn chair
> two lawn chairs
> a very small mattress
> an inner tube
> a sleeping parent
> a rolled up blanket
> a live shark

There are many advantages to not starting off with a real live alligator. Wrestling with a large pillow is much safer, for one thing. For another thing, you don't have to worry about keeping the alligator well fed.

Never, never, never wrestle with an alligator that has not been fed.

That is one of the most important rules of

alligator wrestling. It is also a good rule to apply to a younger brother or sister.

Of course I do not wish to mislead you. You absolutely do not need an alligator in order to practice alligator wrestling, but there most likely will come a time in your training program when trying out your skills on a real live alligator will be desirable, if not necessary. Or necessary, if not desirable. One or the other.

Some people think that the best way to buy an alligator is through the mail. This method of purchasing an alligator does have its advantages. For one thing, you will not have to get close to the alligator. (Is anyone every truly ready to get close to an alligator?) Also, it is a lot of fun watching the mailman trying to stuff a full-grown

alligator into your mailbox. You can learn a lot about wrestling an alligator just by watching a mailman deliver an alligator to your home. Some people, however, when they order an alligator through the mail, complain that they never receive their alligators. There is a reason for this: It is very difficult to find someone brave enough to stick stamps on a real live alligator.

Some experts have told me that the best procedure is to buy an alligator egg and hatch it yourself.

But let's face it. You are going to look pretty silly sitting in your room on an alligator egg. Your friends will ask you to come out and play baseball or tag, and what will you tell them—"Sorry, I can't come out to play right now, I have to sit on this alligator egg until it hatches"? Such a reply will cause no end of problems. People will be calling you up all hours of the day and night, wanting to know if your alligator has hatched yet. Also, if you sit on an alligator egg too long, you will come down with alligator eggitis, a rare skin disease. I say forget the whole thing.

Since, as I may have already mentioned

(were you paying attention?) alligator eggs are not easy to come by, perhaps the best approach is to buy a baby alligator and raise it until it becomes a big alligator (only a sissy wrestles a small alligator). That idea is fine in theory (as many ideas are), but it is useless in practice (as many ideas are). It is useless because you will want to wrestle a wild untamed alligator and not a household pet. Second, you may be a very old man or woman before your alligator is completely grown. For obvious reasons, it is really best to wrestle an alligator when you are very young. If you wait until you are too old to take up this art, your reflexes will be too slow for the delicate turns and maneuvers involved. Also, your voice will have lost some of its youthful power, and so if you have to cry for help, nobody will hear you and the alligator will eat you alive. (When you wrestle an alligator, you always know who the winner is and who the loser is.)

No, I fear there is no way out. Someday you will have to buy a real live alligator and bring it home with you. If you decide on this course of action, then it is merely good manners to tell your parents what you are planning to do.

Never, never, never bring home a live alligator unless you tell your mother first. After all, she may have just waxed the kitchen floor.

Since some parents are less open-minded about alligators than others, you will have to learn how to tell your mother or your father about your new pet. That is why you should read the next chapter very, very carefully.

CHAPTER THREE

How to Tell Your Parents That You Are Bringing Home a Live Wild Alligator So That You Can Practice Your Wrestling Holds

Since the dawn of time, there have been over two million theories about how to bring home a live alligator to your parents without one or both of them going through the roof. Not one of those theories has proven to be useful.

Perhaps you think that you can just sneak a live alligator into your room and leave it there without telling anybody. This sneaky and dishonest approach will work for a few hours, perhaps even for a few months (depending upon how messy your room is), but someday your mother may enter your room and start to clean your bed. When that happens everybody is going to be in trouble. Your mother could be in great trouble, because an alligator does not like to be disturbed. Your alligator could be in trouble if it is sucked up by a vacuum cleaner and carted away with the dust and lint. And you would be in such big trouble that you would be better off moving to the North Pole and living in an igloo. (If you are already living in an igloo at the North Pole, please disregard the previous sentence.) Remember:

It is better to wrestle a starving alligator than it is to face an angry mother.

So forget about trying to sneak an alligator into your room and hoping that nobody will notice it. Don't you think your parents will get suspicious when you take all the food out of the refrigerator every day? (Alligators have to be fed, you understand. If you do not understand that fact now, you will when you own one.)

DAD: Where are you going with all those steaks, son?

SON: Oh, I just thought I'd have a light lunch.

DAD: Seven steaks, two loaves of bread, and fourteen potatoes?

SON: I'm very hungry.

DAD: Well, don't spoil your appetite for supper.

SON: (Breathing a sigh of relief) I won't.

Anyway, I think you can see that hiding an alligator would prove disastrous.

You could give an alligator to your mother for her birthday. There is nothing more heartwarming than to unwrap a beautiful present and to find a full-grown alligator grinning its bright and shiny teeth at you. The secret is to wrap the gift beautifully and carefully. Wrap it in pretty paper and tie it with a colorful ribbon. Yesterday's newspapers and string will not do.

MOTHER: What do we have here?

DAUGHTER: An alligator purse.

MOTHER: But it's so big.

DAUGHTER: I know.

MOTHER: I can't find the zipper.

DAUGHTER: Maybe they forgot to put one in it. You can just put coins and keys in its mouth.

MOTHER: It's pretty. But I don't really need a purse. Why don't you use it?

DAUGHTER: Thanks, Mom.

And off you run to your room with your alligator.

Alternate plan: Pick your mother a bouquet of daisies and hide the alligator among the flowers. Daisies are good flowers for the bouquet because the white petals hide the teeth of the alligator.

You can, of course, try the direct approach. Simply ask your parents if you can bring home a live alligator so you can practice alligator wrestling. Unfortunately, your parents will most likely use the direct approach back at you and tell you "No. A thousand times no. Never."

A better method might be to ask your parents if you can bring home a friend for dinner and then show up with an alligator.

MOTHER: What is this?

SON OR
DAUGHTER: This is an alligator.

FATHER: I thought you said you wanted to bring home a friend for dinner.

SON OR
DAUGHTER: But he is my friend. His name is Freddy. Why can't an alligator be my friend?

Why can't an alligator be my friend? That last question is bound to cause quite a bit of dinner table conversation. Unfortunately some parents are not fond of exploring such intellectual questions in depth, and you will be asked to leave the table and go to your room. The alligator will be left to fend for itself. However, don't worry. Alligators are actually very good at fending for themselves.

By now you probably think that there is

no surefire method of getting an alligator into your home. But this is not so. The surefire method has been saved till last:

Have a close relative give you a live alligator as a present.

There is the solution in a nutshell.

If your ninety-year-old great-grandmother gives you an alligator for your birthday, you certainly can't be expected to give it back or exchange it for a sweater. You'll have to tell your parents, "Gee, Mom and Dad, I can't give this alligator back. It will hurt Grandma's feelings. You don't want me to hurt her feelings, do you?" Of course they don't.

There is only one slight drawback to the above solution. If a close relative gives you an alligator as a pet, you will have to write that person a thank you note. To save you time—time that you can spend wrestling with an alligator—we have written you a thank you note that you can copy. It is on the following page. Copy it exactly, word for word, and your troubles are over. Sort of.

NOTE TO BE WRITTEN AFTER YOU HAVE RECEIVED A REAL LIVE ALLIGATOR FROM A CLOSE RELATIVE

Dear_____, (fill in the blank)
Thank you so much for sending me a real live alligator. It is the perfect size and its teeth are in excellent condition. How did you know that it was something I always wanted?

Love,

(fill in your name here)

P.S. Please excuse the shaky handwriting. Lately I find it very difficult to sit still alone in my room.

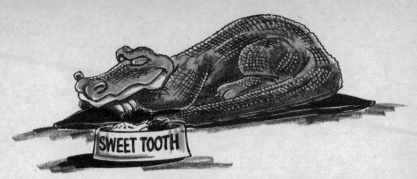

CHAPTER FOUR

What to Name Your Alligator

Now that you have received a live alligator, the first thing to do is give it a name. **Do not take this task lightly. If you give your alligator a name it does not like, you will be in deep trouble.**

Do not name your pet Killer. This will only give your alligator ideas and make your wrestling lessons most difficult.

Some Acceptable Names	Unacceptable Names
Early Tu Bed	Rocky
Swimpty	Rocky II
Deborah	Rocky III
Ima Beast	Rocky IV
Beef Wellington	Rocky V
Sweet Tooth	Rocky VI

CHAPTER FIVE

What to Feed Your Alligator

It has been mentioned before, but it cannot be mentioned too often:

If you are going to wrestle an alligator, it is important to keep your alligator well fed.

The question will often arise, however, just what you should feed your alligator. It really doesn't matter what you feed an alligator, provided you do not feed him any part of yourself. You should also not feed your brother or your sister or anybody you know to an alligator, because young brothers or sisters are very difficult to digest, and you do not want your alligator to have an upset stomach.

Alligators know very little about good nutrition, and, like everybody else, they will eat hamburgers, ice cream, and potato chips if you let them. Sometimes you can get away feeding them spinach smeared with peanut butter. Alligators do not like spinach, lima beans, or cold soups. Thus, if you thought you could get away with feeding your alligator scraps from the table or feeding him or her the foods you yourself do not like—well, you are sadly mistaken.

I believe it also should be pointed out that you (or somebody) will have to cook the alligator's food for him because, of all the animals in the world, alligators make the world's worst cooks. Let an alligator into your kitchen and you will have a real mess on your hands. Alligators like to lie about in a swamp and sing songs such as "I Only Have Teeth for You" or "You Look Good Enough to Eat." They do not like being inside, and they hate being inside kitchens. Alligators very rarely follow recipes and they do not have the patience required to be superior chefs. Thus, if an alligator tries to sell you a bag of homemade chocolate

chip cookies, you would be advised to pass
up the opportunity. Buy your cookies from
Girl Scouts and not from things with
scales. If, however, you meet an alligator
who is also a Girl Scout, then you will have
to make up your own mind.

One final bit of advice:

**Do not put ketchup on any food
served to an alligator**.

The ketchup will most likely remind your
alligator of blood, and blood is the last
thing you want your wrestling opponent to
think about.

CHAPTER SIX

Where to Wrestle with Your Alligator

It is indeed unfortunate that many beginning alligator wrestlers do not give enough thought to the question:

Where is it proper to wrestle with an alligator?

Some amateurs and some uncouth youths believe they can tackle their alligators in just any old setting, but a moment's reflection will reveal that this is not so. You may wrestle with your conscience anywhere you please, but you must pick a good environment for wrestling with your alligator. Wrestling an alligator on a crowded bus, for example, could cause untold inconvenience to passengers trying to get on and off. Nothing is more irritating to a bus rider than missing his or her stop because some selfish person has decided to wrestle an alligator in the aisle.

Also, it is not a good idea to wrestle your alligator in the backseat of your parents' car. If your mother or father is driving you to school, the noise from the backseat will be very distracting and an accident could result. Imagine, if you will, the following scene between a police officer and your mother:

POLICE OFFICER: Why did you go through that red light?

YOUR MOTHER: I was distracted by the alligator in the backseat.

POLICE OFFICER: Sure, lady, sure. I've heard a lot of excuses in my time, but that one really takes the cake.

YOUR MOTHER: But there really is an alligator in the backseat. And my son was there too.

POLICE OFFICER: What do you mean your son *was* there?

YOUR MOTHER: I don't believe he has gotten the hang of properly wrestling an alligator. He lost.

Police officer looks in the backseat of the car.

POLICE OFFICER: Hey, there really is an alligator back there.

YOUR MOTHER: See? I was telling the truth.

POLICE OFFICER: Do you have a license for your alligator?

YOUR MOTHER: No, sir.

POLICE OFFICER: Well, you really are in trouble now. You're under arrest.

Thus, because of one child's thoughtless action, a mother was given a ticket for running a red light and then was taken to jail for having an unlicensed alligator in the backseat. (See next chapter about how to get a license for your alligator.) As for the son, we can only guess what his fate was. The backseat of a car really does not allow enough room to maneuver in. It is very easy for an alligator to take advantage of the novice wrestler in the backseat of a car. Alligator wrestling in a car may prepare you for future dates, but it leads to a very ungraceful wrestling technique.

Some experts feel that movie theaters offer several advantages to a beginning alligator wrestler. The experts point out that movie theaters are often air-conditioned. It is indeed useful to practice alligator wrestling in a cool or cold environment. A sweating alligator is a disgusting sight. Not only is the sight of a sweating alligator unaesthetic, the perspiration makes it difficult for the novice to get a good grip on his or her opponent.

Another advantage of wrestling in a movie theater is lack of direct light. Since alligators are used to bright sunlight (indeed, they prefer sunlight to artificial light) it is easier to take advantage of an alligator in a semidarkened room.

Also there is usually a lot of room in a movie theater. People are staying home and watching television. Therefore, if you go to a movie theater during the day, you might have the entire place to yourself. Thus, in a movie theater, unlike the backseat of an automobile, the novice alligator wrestler* will not be cramped or inhibited by lack of space.

However, before dragging your alligator wrestling companion off to the nearest movie theater for a rigorous workout, you should take note of several important disadvantages.

First, you will have to buy a ticket for your alligator in order to bring him (or her) inside. Very few theater managers are inclined to allow toothed reptiles (including some teenagers) into their movie theaters for free. Since movie tickets cost anywhere from seven dollars on up (unless you can prove that your alligator is under twelve years old, and proving an alligator's age is often difficult), you will soon find yourself out of pocket money. Indeed, if you wrestle with alligators, you may soon find yourself out of pockets. If you wrestle your alligator

---

*Not to be confused with a nervous alligator wrestler.

every day, taking him or her to a movie theater will soon become a major expense. In choosing a proper wrestling site, you should try to choose a place that does not cost money for admission—your own living room, for example. Or a public beach in winter (not in summer when the beach will be crowded).

The most serious disadvantage of movie theaters will be the movies themselves. Many movie theaters show films that are very violent, and I do not believe that you will be doing yourself a service by exposing your alligator to such movies. Scenes of violence will only give your alligator bad ideas. It will also give you bad ideas. Two opponents with bad ideas should not wrestle each other.

If the movie is not a violent one, it could be a comedy. Showing a comedy film to an alligator is a complete waste of time. Alligators have no sense of humor. Alligators do not understand jokes and when they hear people laughing they think the people are laughing at them. Being laughed at causes the alligator to lose his or her temper.

If the movie is not violent and is not a comedy, it most likely will contain sex scenes. Under no circumstances do you want to get your alligator aroused. A lovesick alligator makes sounds that will break your heart. His or her heartrending cries will make it very difficult for you to concentrate upon your wrestling technique.

Even if the film were suitable for an alligator you would still be in a bad position—because the alligator would then rather watch the movie than wrestle with you.

I say **forget taking your alligator to the movies**.

Let us consider some alternative alligator wrestling spaces.

An unoccupied parking space. Parking spaces that are clearly marked with white lines often make good wrestling spaces, but you must remember to put your money in the parking meter every hour or so. Otherwise, you and your alligator could get a ticket. Worse, your alligator could get towed away. There is nothing more embarrassing than watching your wrestling companion being towed down Main Street.

Such a sight is likely to inspire laughter in your friends, and it will take an entire morning or afternoon to get your alligator back from the police. Wrestling in a parking space is also very, very dangerous, because you and your alligator may be down on the ground just at the time someone in a Cadillac decides to park in your space. Being run over by a car can ruin your whole day, and it takes a lot of hard scrubbing to get the tire tracks off your alligator's back.

A classroom at your school may provide alligator wrestling space. Physical education teachers, in fact, may go out of their way to help you with your new sport. Latin teachers, however, may not encourage you to bring your alligator into their classrooms. Every school in the United States has a different policy in regard to alligator wrestling, and so you should check with the principal of your school so that you do not run into any trouble. I, myself, however would never bring an alligator to school. For one thing, alligators do not fit comfortably into any known book bag. For another thing, you will find that other children will want to play with your alligator, thus distracting you and your alligator from the business at hand. Alligator wrestling is a very serious sport. It is not to be taken lightly. If you are going to practice, you should practice in a wide open space, far away from the prying eyes of friends and relatives. Everglades National Park will do. Or Okefenokee Swamp. If you are not within easy walking distance of either of those two places, may I suggest that you build a swamp in your room or on your parents' front porch?

If you build a swamplike setting for your alligator, your alligator will feel right at home. An alligator who feels right at home will make an ideal wrestling companion. But you don't know how to build a swamp in your room, you say? Never fear. Our next chapter tackles—no, not the patiently waiting alligator—but the swamp question head-on.

CHAPTER SEVEN

How to Turn Your Room into a Swamp

Alligators, as I have pointed out, feel right at home in a swamplike setting. Since you, as host or hostess and as a prospective alligator wrestler, wish to do everything in your power to make your wrestling companion feel right at home, it will become necessary for you to turn your room (or your part of a room) into a swamp. If you are anything like a normal child (and if you are reading a book like this I have my doubts), your room is probably only a hop, skip, and a jump away from already being a swamp. For some of you, it is only a hop. For others, a skip. For the majority, merely a short jump.

Don't despair. Anybody can, in a very short time, without any previous experience, turn his or her room into a perfectly acceptable swamp. Remember: A swamp need not be perfect. Perfect swamps do not exist in nature.

What you will need to build a moderate swamp:

2,000 gallons of water (water you have washed your sneakers in will do fine)

43 skunk cabbages

2 skunks (to cover up the terrible smell that will be wafting from your room after your swamp is snugly in place)

200 palm trees (small size)

1,897 blades of saw grass

314 mosquitoes

568 pounds of Spanish moss

63 lily pads

5,675 pounds of dirt

3,241 pebbles

19 rotten logs

8 snakes (optional)

44

Before bringing these swamp ingredients into your room, you should make certain that your floor does not leak. If your floor does leak, your should cover it with plastic.

Obviously if you bring the above-named ingredients into your house all at once your parents could become suspicious. If they ask what you are doing, tell them you are working on a science project for school. After all, you could learn something from this undertaking and you could turn it into a science project if you wish.

I am building (or working on) a science project—that is the best excuse in the world a person can have for doing any weird thing.

The best way to get all the ingredients up to your room is to smuggle the materials in little by little. A pocketful of dirt here, a rotten log there, a few pounds of Spanish moss pressed between the pages of a math book. Obviously such a procedure takes a long time, but that is why it is important to begin alligator wrestling at a very early age. By the time you have the swamp built, you will have grown and matured.

Alligator wrestling is not for the immature!

Bring the dirt in first. Add water. Plant the trees and swamp cabbages and saw grass. If you cannot locate saw grass, you can use real saws. Add the pebbles and the rotten logs. Put the lily pads on top of the water. Release the mosquitoes. And above all:

Keep the door to your room closed at all times.

CHAPTER EIGHT

What to Wear while
Wrestling Your Alligator

By now you are probably anxious to begin alligator wrestling, but there really is no need to rush blindly into the matter. Alligators will be around for a long time (we hope) and so too will be the opportunity to wrestle with them. The main thing is to be patient and to look after each detail, step by step. Improper planning has ruined the career, not to mention the health, of many a budding alligator wrestler.

Remember: Prior planning prevents putrid performance.

Memorize that rule and you will be well on your way to success in life.

The next detail we need to consider is: *fashion*. What do the well-dressed alligator and alligator wrestler wear? A nude alligator is a sight that most of us can do without, so I hope you will spend some time in selecting the correct wrestling costume for your opponent and yourself. Cut-off jeans and a white T-shirt will only brand you as a rank amateur.

Capes—you should wear a cape, because when you see superheroes flying about the sky, they are always wearing capes. Thus, if an alligator sees you in a cape, he or she may get the idea that you are a superhero also. It is always good to wear clothing and accessories that will inspire fear in your opponent. For this reason, you should wear the cape and not your alligator. Giving an alligator a cape is only adding fuel to the fire.

Your alligator should wear a brightly colored phosphorescent tank suit. Whatever the alligator wears should glow in the dark. You will find this very useful if you ever have to wrestle an alligator at night. You, on the other hand (or claw), should wear dark colors that do not glow.

In other words, the principle for dressing for an alligator wrestling match is:

The alligator should be easy to see; you should not be easy to see.

Believe me, you are going to need every advantage you can get.

In addition to a cape, you should consider wearing a mask. I advise this, not because I think your natural face is ugly, but because a mask also inspires fear in your opponent. Wearing masks will help you to

assume a number of different identities. Thus, if you lose (which we hope will not happen) an alligator wrestling match, you can return for a rematch as somebody else. Yes, masks are definitely useful.

Another good reason for wearing a mask is to cover up your embarrassment in case you lose your wrestling match. If you have worn a mask during your match, then you can still walk down the streets of your hometown and hold your head high.

It is, however, not a good idea to lose an alligator wrestling match.

If you have long hair, you should think about having it cut off. You do not want the alligator to pull on your hair. You will find such pulling quite painful.

All your clothes should be tight fitting. You do not want to get into a wrestling ring with loose-fitting clothes. In other words, the simple dress code is:

Do not wear anything that will allow your opponent to get a good grip on you.

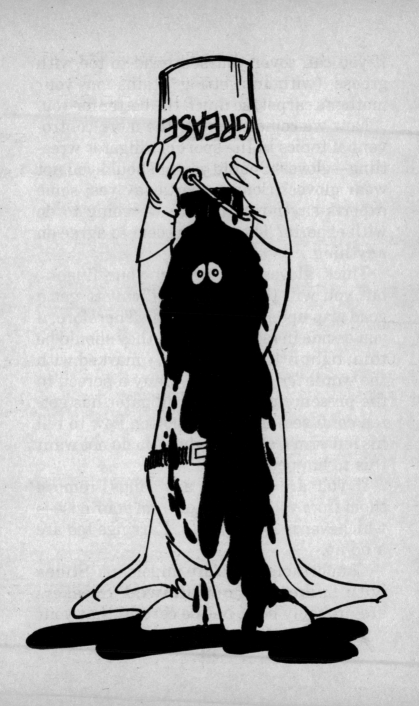

If you can cover yourself head to toe with grease (without getting stains on your mother's carpet) so much the better for you.

Now we come to one of the more controversial topics in the sport of alligator wrestling—gloves. Should you or should you not wear gloves? Some experts say yes; some experts say no. What are we going to do with experts? They never seem to agree on anything.

Thick gloves will protect your fingers, but you will then find it difficult to get a good grip upon your opponent. Therefore, if you decide in favor of gloves, they should be thin, tight fitting, and clearly marked with the words *left* and *right*. Many a person in the presence of an angry alligator has gotten confused and has forgotten how to tell his left arm from his right. You do not want this to happen to you.

If you are wearing any rings, remove them from your fingers or from your nose— whichever is appropriate. Earrings too are a no-no.

Comfortable shoes are important. **Shoes with spikes are not allowed**. Sneakers are probably best, but be certain that your shoelaces are carefully tied. Once again, be certain that your shoes are clearly marked *left* or *right*, or *right* and *left* (as the case may be). If you get so excited that you put your shoes on the wrong feet, you will feel pain even before you start to wrestle, and the main reason you are studying this manual is so you can **minimize your pain as much as possible under the circumstances**.

All your clothing should be tight fitting (but not so tight that you cannot breathe. If you cannot breathe, you will most likely lose your wrestling match. Good breathing—actually, any breathing at all—is helpful to an alligator wrestler).

In closing, I shall simply repeat an idea that was touched upon briefly earlier in this chapter: whatever you do it is important that your alligator wear clothing also. Never—and I repeat this—**never, never wrestle a naked alligator**! A naked alligator will only embarrass you, and if you are embarrassed, you will have a difficult time concentrating upon your wrestling.

CHAPTER NINE

Alligators and the Age-Old
Cheerleader Question

Before you begin your first alligator wrestling match, you will have to decide whether you will want cheerleaders on the sidelines to cheer you on. If you have cheerleaders, however, it is only fair for your alligator to have cheerleaders on his or her side also. I guess the answer to the question will depend upon whether you have cheerleaders in your family or not. The answer also may depend on your ability to find pom-poms and letter sweaters for the reptile side. You should be warned, however, that there is nothing sadder than seeing alligator cheerleaders attempting to do backflips and nose stands. Alligators are good at wrestling, but are simply ridiculous when they attempt somersaults. As a great philosopher once said, "A somersaulting alligator is worth two in the bush." What the philosopher meant is anybody's guess, but that is the way philosophers are.

However, should you decide to use cheerleaders to keep your spirits up, then you should have your cheerleaders use the following cheer:

> Ooooga oooooga ooopga
> Chumlex chumlex chumlex opga
> Gooobi gopy peeetie pie
> Ooooga oooooga ooopga

That cheer may not, at first glance, make any sense to you, but an alligator will recognize it right away. It is the equivalent of an alligator lullaby, and if your cheerleaders present it softly with correct emphasis (on the final syllable of each word), there is a good chance that the cheer will render your opponent sleepy. You will find there are times when it is of great advantage to wrestle a sleepy or sleeping alligator.

An alligator that is wide awake can be a pesky creature. In addition to using the above-mentioned cheer, it's not a bad idea to give your alligator a glass of warm milk before starting to wrestle.

Since you will be spending a lot of your free time practicing your wrestling skills and keeping yourself and your alligator in shape, there is no doubt that you will find it difficult to keep up with your schoolwork. Hence, it may not be a bad idea to use cheerleaders to keep you up to date on various subjects. Thus, a typical sequence of cheers could go:

I-N-S-E-C-T—that's how to spell insect.

Nine times eight is seventy-two.

M-A-N-A-D-O, Manado is a seaport in northeast Celebes in Indochina.

An octopus has eight legs.

P-O-N-I-A-R-D is how to spell poniard.*

---

*A typical cheer used by the opposing side—i.e., the alligators—frequently consists of variations of lines from *Hamlet*. For example, "To cheer or not to cheer, that is the question." This goes to show that alligators are a lot more literate and ambivalent than most persons (especially wrestlers) suspect. The publishers of this book thought that you might be interested in knowing that.

In fact, it might not be a bad idea to have someone on the sidelines reading you short stories, poems, and plays so you don't flunk English.

No matter how much you enjoy alligator wrestling as a sport or hobby, remember it is very difficult to make your living at it. Thus, you should still keep up with your schoolwork.

Always remind your cheerleaders **not to jump too close to the alligator**. It is one thing to hear inspiring cheers from the sidelines. Such cheers will lift your spirits and help you fight a good fight. It is quite another thing to hear a muffled cheer coming from inside the alligator. Such a cheer is not at all inspiring or uplifting. It will also give your alligator an added weight advantage.

CHAPTER TEN

How to Tell an Alligator
from a Crocodile

You are now ready to begin your first workout. You go into your room (or swamp, as it is now) and you square off with your alligator. You look your alligator square in the face and what do you see? Do you see an animal that has a narrow snout? You look even closer (I advise you to look through binoculars or a telescope) and you notice that the fourth tooth in each side of the lower jaw is visible when the mouth is closed.

Are you ready to begin?

No, you are not. Absolutely not. Because if you can see that fourth tooth protruding, you have made a big mistake. You have brought home a crocodile and not an alligator. Get that crocodile out of your room before it is too late.

Why?

Because there is a big difference in the personalities of alligators and crocodiles. They may look alike, but they are *not* alike. Alligators can be friendly; crocodiles are mean.

A crocodile will as soon attack you as look at you.

Do not, under any conditions, attempt to wrestle a crocodile. Alligators will give you enough trouble.

CHAPTER ELEVEN

On Entering the Ring Where a Live Alligator Awaits You

Before entering a ring to wrestle a live alligator, you should decide upon a battle cry, or a cry of attack. If you can give forth a blood-piercing cry you may throw some fear into the alligator's heart, thus gaining a slight edge in the opening moments of the contest.

Of course, in order to acquire a blood-piercing cry (you may want to look at old Tarzan movies to get an idea of what I have in mind) you will need to spend hours and hours screaming at the top of your lungs. It is not a good idea to practice your bloodcurdling yell during a math exam, while brushing your teeth (you might swallow your toothbrush), or at three o'clock in the morning if you happen to have parents or neighbors.

There really is only one good place to practice your alligator wrestling cry and that is in the middle of the Sahara. Therefore, you are going to have to earn the money to get a plane ticket to go to the Sahara. (Don't ask me where it is. I am not a geographer.)

If you cannot reach the Sahara, you can substitute one of the following places:

Mount Everest

Antarctica

A motion picture theater showing a Serbo-Croatian romantic comedy without any subtitles.

CHAPTER TWELVE

What Not to Do While
Wrestling an Alligator

Before going into what you should do while wrestling your alligator (that will be the next chapter. Maybe.) it is important to understand **what not to do**. Here are a few things to be avoided:

1. When getting into a wrestling ring with an alligator, do not put your hands over your eyes and start to cry. This will only give the alligator bad ideas.

2. Do not chew bubble gum during a wrestling match with an alligator. Popping bubbles will make the alliga-

tor think it is being shot at and then you will have a difficult time carrying on any sort of physical contact.

3. DO NOT TURN YOUR BACK ON YOUR ALLIGATOR. (This rule is so important that I have put it in capital letters.) When taking off your cape (see chapter 8) face the alligator and, above all, do not take your eyes off him or her.

4. Do not smile at your opponent. A smile could mislead the alligator into thinking that you are only fooling around, when you really mean business.

CHAPTER THIRTEEN

How to Tickle an Alligator

Forget it. Alligators are not ticklish. It's not the alligator's fault. If you grew up in a swamp (as now you are, if you made your room into one), you would lose your sense of humor too. After all, as you are finding out, swamps do not provide much amusement. In most swamps, it is difficult even to find a decent fast hamburger stand. No video arcades. No libraries overflowing with books such as this one.

No wonder alligators are in foul moods most of the time.

OK, OK, I know that being ticklish has very little in common with possessing a sense of humor, but that scientific insight

applies only to humans, not to reptiles. There are, in fact, only two or three examples of proverbial wisdom that apply to both humans and reptiles.

One is: A watched alligator rarely boils. I forget what the other two insights are.

Still, I warn you—do not waste your valuable time tickling an alligator's feet, tickling its armpits, or blowing into its ear.

Alligators are not ticklish and they do not laugh at jokes.

If you don't believe me, you can find out the hard way, but it is the aim of this book to help save you time and embarrassment. But go ahead. Walk up to your alligator and say:

Who was that lady I just saw you with?
That was no lady. That was my wife.

or

Why did the chicken cross the road?
To get to the other side.

See if that gets you a laugh. Or a smile.

CHAPTER FOURTEEN

The Basic Moves

At long last, we are ready to discuss the basic moves that open up an entirely new world to you, plus exciting career opportunities.

Remember: You can (and should) practice these basic moves on a large green pillow before moving on to a real live alligator.

Do not confuse your alligator with a pillow. If you are having a problem getting to sleep at night perhaps it is because you are sleeping on an alligator.

Move 1: The Basic Closet Retreat Move

In order for the basic closet retreat move to work, you will need a closet in your room/ swamp. If you do not have such a closet, you should stop reading, go to your nearest lumberyard, and start building one. Once you have your closet in place, you will be ready to continue.

You run over to your alligator, give out with your blood- or milk-curdling yell, bop the alligator on the tip of his nose, and then you dash into your closet and slam the door. (**Make certain you have drilled enough air holes in the door or you may suffocate**.)

You stay in the closet until the alligator has fallen asleep or lost interest. When the alligator has fallen asleep, you may declare yourself the winner of the match.

Move 2: The Move to Another City

You enter the ring, remove your cape, give forth with your milk shake—curdling

yell, run forward as fast as you can, run right across the entire length of your alligator and out the door. You keep on running to the nearest airport and take the first plane to Alaska. (If you are reading this book in Alaska, take the first plane to Mexico City.) Stay in hiding until the alligator's temper has time to cool down. Remember:

It takes a long time for an alligator's temper to cool. Alligators have a very good memory and do not forget a slight.

(If you don't believe me—read *Peter Pan*. Or was that about a crocodile?)

If you cannot fly to another city, you can disguise yourself as a duck and waddle around the backyard for a couple of weeks. You may get embarrassed, however, when your friends start throwing you bread crumbs.

Move 3: The Half Nelson

Some people have written that the wrestling lock known as the half nelson got

started when a boy named Nelson leaped onto the back of a hungry alligator. But that story is sheer nonsense. The half nelson is a respected wrestling hold. Unfortunately, it is not respected by alligators. Therefore, you will have to use the whole Nelson. To use the whole Nelson, simply find a friend named Nelson, bring him up to your room, and push him toward the alligator. While the alligator is looking at the whole Nelson, you use the famous hammerlock (see next move, 4) and subdue your opponent.

At the conclusion of the alligator wrestling match, you may also need a special hold to subdue a very angry Nelson.

Move 4: The Hammerlock

If you see an alligator carrying a hammer, grab the hammer away from him or her and lock the hammer in your closet. It is hard enough to fight an alligator who is unarmed; an alligator carrying a hammer is unbeatable.

On the other hand, if your alligator is good with a hammer, you might call off the wrestling match and ask your alligator to build a few bookcases for you. If you need books for your bookcases, you cannot go wrong by buying a few hundred copies of *Alligator Wrestling and You*. A person cannot have too many copies of such a necessary reference work.

CONCLUSION

Now that you have studied the fine art of alligator wrestling and have learned the basic moves, you may feel ready to take on the whole world. Remember, however, that the world is not the same thing as an alligator. One has sharper teeth. Also,

Do not try any of these moves out on a real live alligator until you have practiced, practiced, practiced.

When you reach 105 years of age you may be ready to tackle a live alligator.

Do not rush in where angels fear to tread.

Of course, you can always go back and read this book again. One can never have too much knowledge.

STRANGER THAN FICTION

by MELVIN BERGER

ASTOUND YOUR FRIENDS
WITH INCREDIBLE, LITTLE-KNOWN FACTS ABOUT...

KILLER BUGS　　　　76036-3/$3.50 US/$4.25 Can

More people are killed by insects than by all other animals combined—including sharks and snakes.

DINOSAURS　　　　76052-5/$2.95 US/$3.50 Can

Dinosaurs are the largest, most magnificent and most terrifying creatures that ever roamed the Earth.

MONSTERS　　　　76053-3/$2.95 US/$3.50 Can

Do creatures like Big Foot and the Abominable Snowman really exist?

SEA MONSTERS　　　　76054-1/$2.95 US/$3.50 Can

Unlike the shark in *Jaws*, this book is about the real living sea monsters that swim the waters of the world.

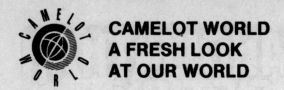

CAMELOT WORLD
A FRESH LOOK
AT OUR WORLD

THE MYSTERIOUS CAT 76038-X/$2.95 US/$3.50 Can
by Elizabeth Garrick

HOT MACHINES 76039-8/$2.95 US/$3.50 Can
by Gregory Pope

SECRETS OF THE SAMURAI 76040-1/$2.95 US/$3.50 Can
by Carol Gaskin

A KID'S GUIDE TO HOW TO SAVE THE PLANET
76041-X/$2.95 US/$3.50 Can
by Billy Goodman

GREAT DISASTERS 76043-6/$2.95 US/$3.50 Can
by David Keller

DOLLS 76044-4/$2.95 US/$3.50 Can
by Vivian Werner

UFOS AND ALIENS 76045-2/$2.95 US/$3.50 Can
by William R. Alschuler

A KID'S GUIDE TO HOW TO SAVE THE ANIMALS
76651-5/$2.99 US/$3.50 Can
by Billy Goodman

SECRETS OF THE DOLPHINS 76046-0/$2.95 US/$3.50 Can
by Diana Reiss

WHAT IS WAR? WHAT IS PEACE? 76704-X/$2.95 US/$3.50 Can
by Richard Rabinowitz